The Trickster

Poems for Very Clever Children & Silly Adults

Daniel Klawitter

Illustrations by Robyn Crowell

White Bird Publications
P.O. Box 90145
Austin, Texas 78709
http://www.whitebirdpublications.com

This is a work of poetry by Daniel Klawitter.

ISBN: 978-1-63363-396-4
LCCN: 2019941105

PRINTED IN THE UNITED STATES OF AMERICA

Dedication

This book is fondly dedicated to the young and the young at heart…especially all the geeks and freaks and weirdos who love poetry.

p.s.: If you love poetry so much, why don't you go ahead and marry it?

Acknowledgments

Grateful acknowledgment is due the editors of the following publications, magazines, and websites for publishing the poems indi-
cated below, sometimes in previous versions:

Fellowship & Fairydust: "I Want to Go to Narnia"

Rainy Day Poems: "Babies," "Geeks & Freaks & Weirdos," "I
Don't Want to Be a Princess," "I Dreamed I Saw Shel Silverstein,"
"Last to Be Picked for the Team," "Mmmm…Catfish!" "Rock
Stars," "The Bing-Bong-Boo," "The Orc with No Fork," "The
Land of Ice Cream," "The Lonesome Scarecrow," "The Monster
Hunters," "The Mystery of Pickles," and "The Whacky Wizard"

Social Justice Poetry: "Discovery, 1492"

Stinkwaves Magazine: "An Apple a Day" and "The Trickster"

The Caterpillar: "Haters"

The Poet Community: "Wild!"

VerseWrights: "Poetry in Yo Face" and "The Book of St. Albans"

Thanks also to poet Robert Schechter for your careful reading of
The Trickster in manuscript form and your helpful suggestions.
And a deep bow of gratitude to Robyn Crowell for being my col-
laborator by providing such delightful and whimsical illustrations
for this book.

Contents

The Trickster

Coyote creeps through raindrops
And slinks between the trees—
So crafty and so cunning
With a trick up every sleeve.

He likes the taste of porcupine
And has a sense of humor.
He gifted fire to humankind,
According to one rumor.

He's neither wolf nor dog,
But something in between.
Perhaps, he is a demigod
Who isn't what he seems.

The Lonesome Scarecrow

A farmer stuck me in his field
To scare off all the crows.
It's lonesome here amongst the corn,
As you might well suppose.

He dressed me like a human
But I'm only made of straw.
And all day long I hear the crows:
Caw-caw! Caw-caw! Caw-caw!

There's no one I can talk to
For miles and miles around.
I cannot move my arms or legs;
I'm fastened to the ground.

I'd love to play a game of tag
And run through rows of corn
Instead of being stuck up here,
So lonesome and forlorn.

As I stare at the horizon,
I protect the crops from harm.
The king of all that I survey:
The fields, the house, the barn.

But heavy is my burlap head.
My hat is not a crown.
I'm such a lonely scarecrow.
Won't you come and take me down?

Wild!

I like to feel the sunshine
And the grass beneath my feet.
I like to see the wily weeds
Peek up through hard concrete.

Some things we just cannot contain:
The wind, the truth, the sky—
Animals we can barely tame,
No matter how we try.

The world's an endless mystery
By which I am beguiled.
So I sing of liberation—
I sing of all things wild!

I Want to Go to Narnia

I want to go to Narnia
Where the animals can speak.
I want to meet King Aslan
And the mouse named Reepicheep.

I want to ride a centaur,
Which truly would be wondrous!
I want to cheer up Puddleglum
And have tea with Mr. Tumnus.

I want to go to Narnia
Where the River Shribble flows,
But the wardrobe in my house
Is only filled with clothes.

Geeks & Freaks & Weirdos

This poem is for all the losers
Who have never won a trophy:
The beggars who can't be choosers—
The awkward & the lonely.
The geeks & freaks & weirdos
Who so often are harassed.
I think you all are heroes,
And the first shall be the last!
So try to count your blessings,
Though most days you may feel cursed.
Here ends the final lesson
When the last shall be the first.

Stink Bomb

Last week my poo poo spoke to me
From the bottom of the commode:
"If you dare to flush me down
Instead I will explode!"

I did not want that to happen—
It sounded like a threat.
So still it lurks and talks to me;
I haven't flushed it yet.

Last to Be Picked for the Team

I am a fan of sports,
Though I've never been athletic.
I don't run around in shorts;
Some say I look pathetic!

I don't want to pull a hamstring,
Or suffer a head concussion.
I'm not a fan of anything
Involving armpit sweat production.

I Dreamed I Saw Shel Silverstein

I dreamed I saw Shel Silverstein
Alive as you or me.
His head was bare of any hair
As he hugged The Giving Tree.

I begged him for a song or two—
He picked up his guitar,
And sang about "A Boy Named Sue,"
Whose father had a scar.

And then we had a "Hug O' War"
Like the very best of friends.
I dreamed I saw Shel Silverstein
Down Where the Sidewalk Ends.

The Land of Ice Cream

I've found the land of ice cream
Where chocolate rivers flow…
And mountains of vanilla
Above the Rocky Road.

Strawberry fields forever—
Banana Split surprise,
Clouds of soft marshmallows
Afloat in sherbet skies.

A forest made of cookie dough
Will cause your lips to smack.
I've found the land of ice cream,
And I'm never coming back.

If Your Butt...

If your butt were on your front
Instead of your behind,
I think you'd find it difficult
To sit with peace of mind.

For if your butt was on your front
It wouldn't be perfection.
You'd pass your gas a different way
In the opposite direction.

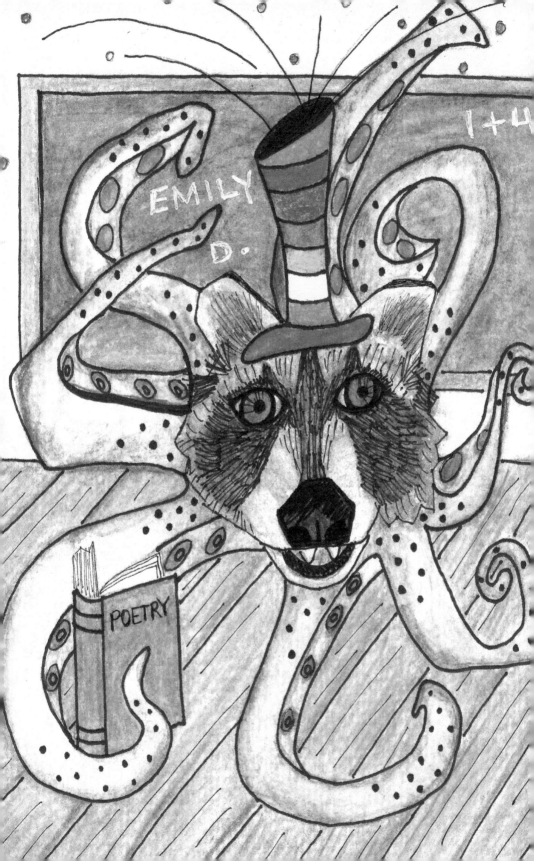

The Bing-Bong-Boo

I must tell you of the Bing-Bong-Boo
In the basement of my school—
A mystic, magic creature
Who is kind and never cruel.

With the body of an octopus
And a face like a raccoon,
I don't know how he got here,
But he isn't leaving soon.

He loves reciting poetry
To anyone who will listen.
His favorite poet in the world
Is Emily E. Dickinson.

Why is he called the Bing-Bong-Boo?
I'm not sure—in fact, I'm clueless!
I just know he loves poetry,
And he comes from Massachusetts.

Poetry in Yo Face

If I feel physically as if the top of my head were taken off,
I know that is poetry.
                                        —Emily Dickinson

If hope is the thing with feathers
Like the Myth of Amherst said—
Then poems are words like birds,
Nesting in your head, singing sweetly
Or chirping curses.
As likely to peck your eyes out
As dazzle you with verses.

To Each His Own

Jimmy likes burritos—
Burritos filled with bugs!
Centipedes & millipedes,
And beetles, worms, & slugs.
All kinds of creepy crawlies—
He says they are delicious.
He loves their chewy bodies,
But I find his tastes suspicious.

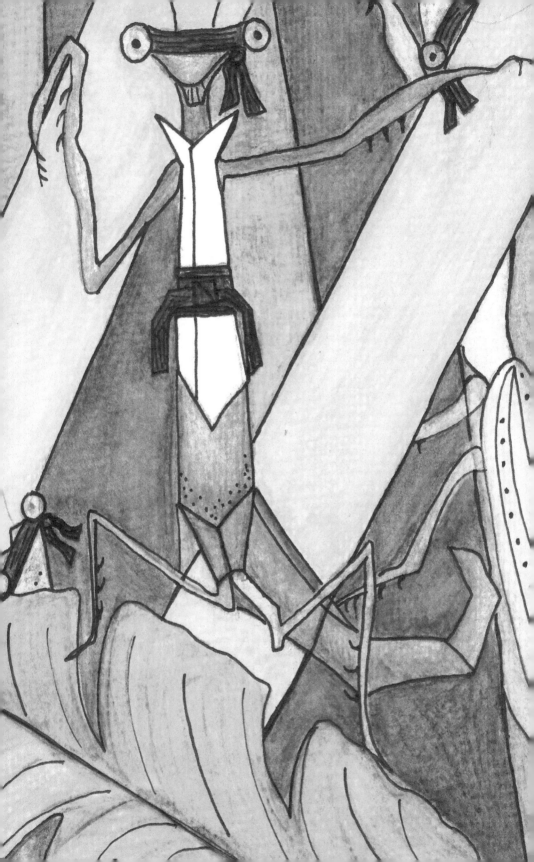

The Praying Mantis

I think the neatest bug of all
Must be the Praying Mantis—
They know kung fu, and it may be true
That they used to rule Atlantis!

They might resemble leaves or sticks—
These masters of disguise.
They can see in true 3-D
(Why not? They have five eyes!)

It's so cool how they can turn their head
A hundred and eighty degrees!
These carnivores who live outdoors
Have lots of expertise.

And the lady Praying Mantis
Can have a thousand youngsters,
But she sometimes eats the father,
From his head down to his dumpster.

Rain, Rain Go Away

I forgot my dang umbrella,
And now I'm drenched in rain.
I'm a moist and soggy fella
From my shoes up to my brain!

The rain came down like spittle,
And now I'm soaked in water.
They said it would rain a little—
But instead it rained a lotta!

Discovery, 1492

Columbus was no hero,
Just a guy who got real lost—
Landed in the Bahamas
And launched a holocaust.

The Indians there were peaceful.
He enslaved them just the same.
And became a brutal tyrant—
The lust for gold inflamed his veins.

As Governor of the Indies
For seven terrible years,
He helped to start the slave trade
And cut off people's ears.

This genocidal maniac
Was quite uncivilized.
I wish his ships had sunk at sea,
And he never had arrived.

The Homeless

You might see them on a corner—
Holding up a sign,
With missing teeth & bleary eyes
And clothing caked with grime.

Some people get embarrassed
And turn their eyes away.
Some people hand them money
For food just for today.

Some people who you wouldn't guess
Are living in their cars—
While some rich folks live in mansions,
And have champagne with caviar.

It's a complicated issue—
Then again, maybe it's not.
A person is more than what they own,
But some of us forgot.

Haters

Some folks are good at hating.
It's all they've ever known.
They learned it from their parents
And practiced it at home.

I'm not sure why they do it,
But those who feel compelled
To hate those who are different
May really hate themselves.

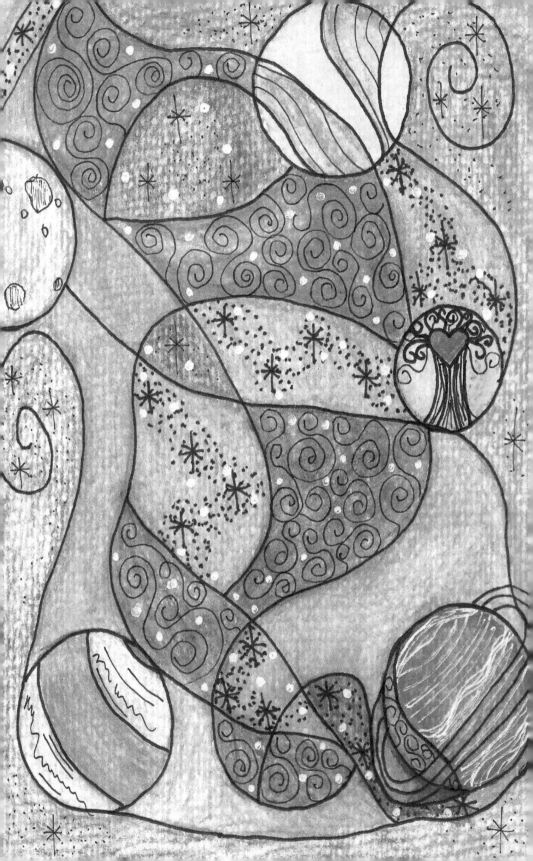

A Different World

I dream of planets far away—
And galaxies that spin
Far beyond the Milky Way
Where no one's ever been.

And there among the quasars,
The black holes and the comets—
I'll find a planet just like ours,
But with better economics.

A world where there's no rich or poor,
But everyone has enough.
A world where there is no more war,
And humans matter more than stuff.

Mmmm...Catfish!

My favorite food is catfish,
And I like to eat it fried.
It purrs inside my tummy,
So delicious and divine!

But I hate the taste of dogfish—
It makes me want to retch,
Then scratch myself behind the ear
And play a game of fetch.

Rock Stars

Mary had a little lamb
Whose fleece was black as coal.
They got together, formed a band,
And played loud rock and roll!

Mary was the singer.
The lamb played his guitar.
With a rabbit for a drummer,
They soon became big stars.

With a rooster on the bass,
The quartet was complete.
They played their songs all night long
With a funky, farm-fresh beat!

Their concerts were amazing!
They sold out every show.
From the U.S.A. to Europe
And even Tokyo.

They became a world sensation
That everyone admired,
And now they live in Florida,
Happily retired.

I Don't Want to Be a Princess

I don't want to be a princess
And have to wear a dress.
I'd rather be a writer,
For that's what I do best.

I like to think up stories
Where girls don't need a prince—
Because we're just as brave as them
And have more common sense.

Babies

Have you ever seen a baby?
They look like little blobs.
All they do is eat and cry—
The dirty, lazy slobs!

I'm glad I'm not a baby—
A helpless, dumb buffoon.
My mom just said to stop this poem
And go clean up my room.

An Apple a Day

An apple a day
Keeps the doctor away,
Unless your Doc is famished.
Then in that case
They'll stuff their face
Like giant, woolly mammoths!
They'll never leave your house
Till they've eaten all your fruit!
Those apple eating doctors
Will leave you destitute.

The Mystery of Pickles

I always thought that pickles
Grew on a pickle tree.
But a cucumber will tell you,
"The pickle comes from me!"

How can they taste so different
And yet still be the same?
The secret's in the vinegar;
Fermentation is to blame!

The cucumber takes a bath
In a salty, acidic brine.
It stays in there for 7 days
And comes out tasting fine.

Cucumbers when left untreated,
Are something I abhor,
But when they turn to pickles,
They are better than before.

Bossy Lisa Lou

"You are not the boss of me!"
I screamed at Lisa Lou—
When for the hundred thousandth time
She told me what to do.
Rules are quite important
To every aspect of her life.
She's like a little Sergeant—
It creates a lot of strife!
I've counted up her orders,
And there are a hundred million.
O bossy, bossy Lisa…
You're not the boss of this civilian!

Litterbug

You should never, never, ever
Throw your trash into the street—
Especially not your bubble gum.
It sticks to people's feet!

And definitely not a diaper
That is filled with poop and pee—
That's totally disgusting!
I'm sure that you agree.

And certainly not that wrapper
From the burger you devoured—
It ends up on the sidewalk
Or stuck in trees and flowers.

Trash goes in the garbage!
So do not be a thug—
If you throw it on the sidewalk,
You're a dirty litterbug.

The Monster Hunters

Bobby caught a vampire
Inside a vampire trap.
Susan caught a mummy
She proceeded to unwrap.
The mummy was very brittle,
And quickly it did crumble.
The vampire changed into a bat,
And with a chilling chuckle
He mocked the silly children
For their efforts which had failed.
But he flew into a wooden stake
And was suddenly impaled.
Then with a dying whisper,
He cursed his lousy luck—
To be caught by the brother & sister,
Without a drop of blood to suck.

Sebastian

No matter what your stature is; how tall you are or not—
You can always go out fishing in your favorite fishing spot!
Just like my friend Sebastian, who was born in Dusseldorf.
From head to toe he's four feet four. You might say he's a dwarf.
His favorite fish is halibut, but he's also fond of flounder.
And a better angler in all the world I never have encountered!
His fishing rod is not that long, but perfectly proportioned—
Just like my friend Sebastian, out fishing on the ocean.

The Orc with No Fork

One day when I was walking,
I was accosted by an Orc,
Who wanted to eat me piece by piece,
But he did not have a fork.
With great relief I ran away,
And I did so none too soon.
For in the distance I heard him howl:
"Come back! I have a spoon!"

Holy Guacamole!

Do you like guacamole?
It's made from avocados.
It's pure and good and holy.
I eat it with bravado!

I take my gold tortilla chip,
And I scoop up all the green:
It's such a creamy, savory dip—
But my dad says I'm not clean!

For every time I eat it,
I make a mighty mess.
My sister throws a hissy fit
Because I ate it all…I guess.

Grocery Shopping

I bet that you have never seen
A walking, talking tangerine.
Like the one on aisle 17
Speaking with a can of beans.

The can of beans said: "You're sweet & tart!"
Tangerine replied: "You make folks fart!"
And then they laughed, which warmed my heart.
So I put them in our grocery cart.

When we got home, I took them out,
But no more did they talk or shout.
It seems the truth beyond all doubt
Is they were slain by Brussels sprouts.

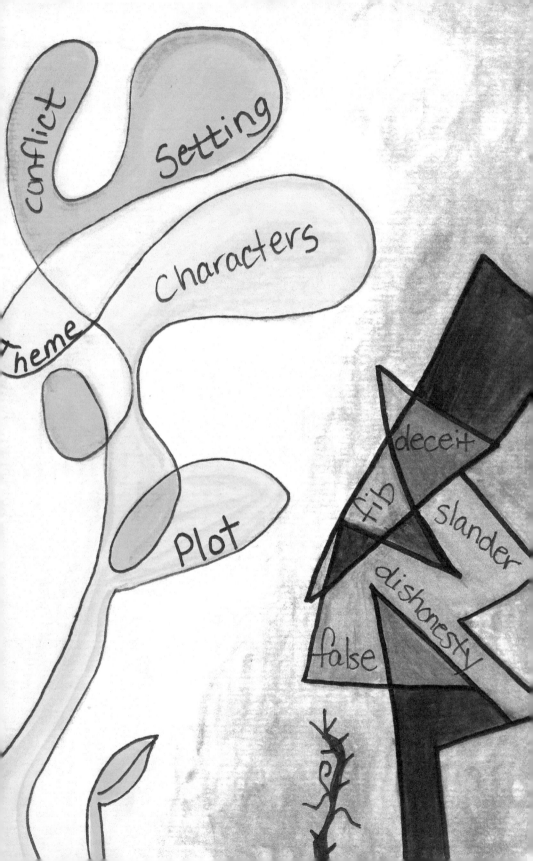

A Story and a Lie

There is a crucial difference
Between a story and a lie.
A fable may be fiction,
But with a greater truth inside.

But a lie is a deception
For the liar's own protection,
And it spreads like an infection
If left without correction!

So, feel free to tell a story
To Jack and Jill and Sid,
But don't forget the difference
Between a story and a fib.

Bad Piggy

Oh piggish, piggish piggy bank
Made somewhere in Nevada.
I put my pennies in you—
Now it seems that I have nada.

Oh piggish, piggish piggy bank
I never could have guessed—
That you would steal my pennies
And make me so distressed!

I had planned to buy some candy
With all the pennies I had saved,
And that's what would have happened.
But my piggy misbehaved.

Careful What You Wish For

I wish I had a robot
That would do all of my chores:
Clean my room and mow the lawn
And take the trash outdoors.
But if I had a robot
And it did all my work,
I'd grow up spoiled and rotten
And probably be a jerk.

The Whacky Wizard

I am a whacky wizard
With whacky wizard ways.
I feast on chicken gizzards
And jars of mayonnaise.

I change grown-ups into ketchup
And kids to tater tots.
Then I mix them all together
And put them in a pot.

For I am the kind of wizard
Whose magic power is food.
I drink milkshakes made of lizards.
I'm a whacky wizard dude.

My neighbors are very frightened
Of the wicked things I do.
I change their pets to hot dogs
And have a barbecue.

But wizardry is lonely
And my food is much too rich.
It's not much fun to eat alone,
I guess I'll find a witch!

The Book of St. Albans

A murder of crows—
A gaggle of geese.
In poetry and prose—
An ancient masterpiece!
A parliament of owls
Or perhaps a scream of swifts.
You can feel it in your bowels:
Such luscious artifice!

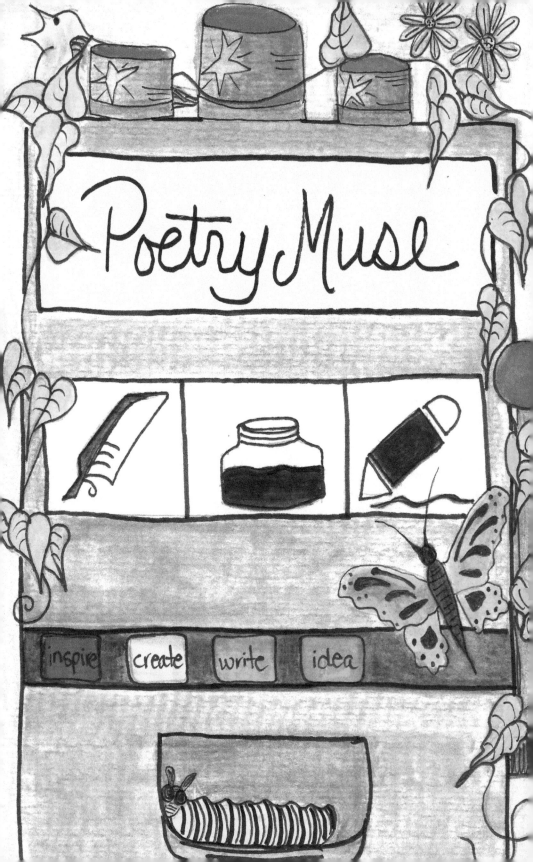

The Fickle, Fickle Muse

Poetry isn't easy—
No matter what they say.
For the muse she sometimes giveth,
And she sometimes takes away.

About the Illustrator:

Robyn Crowell is a visual artist and a designer of custom jewelry and accessories. She studied Theater, Fine Arts, Design, and Studio Painting at Stephen F. Austin State University, Wharton College, and Houston Community College. She is also a graduate of Excellence for Leadership in Nonprofits from The George Foundation. Robyn lives just outside Houston, TX with her husband and two cats. She is the proud mother of two grown daughters who are also artists.

CPSIA information can be obtained
at www.ICGtesting.com
Printed in the USA
BVHW061917010420
576572BV00006B/159

9 781633 633964